New Vanguard • 81

German Heavy Cruisers 1939–45

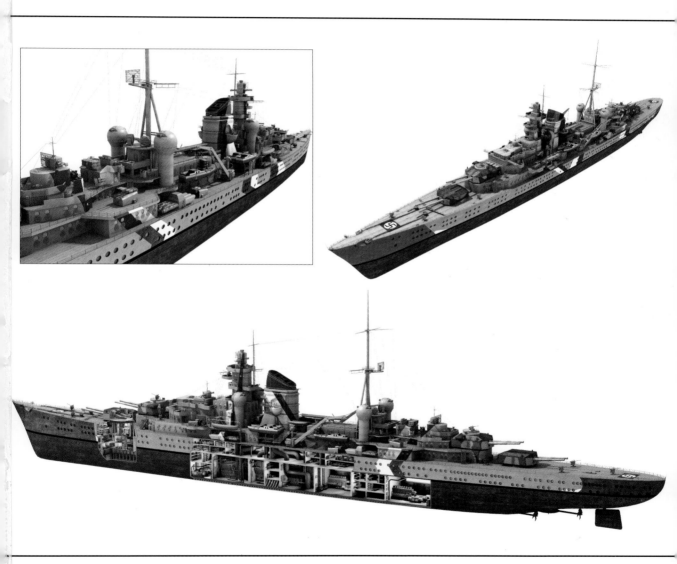

Gordon Williamson • Illustrated by Ian Palmer

First published in Great Britain in 2003 by Osprey Publishing, Elms Court, Chapel Way, Botley, Oxford OX2 9LP, United Kingdom.
Email: info@ospreypublishing.com

ISBN 1 84176 502 3

Editor: Simone Drinkwater
Design: Melissa Orrom Swan
Index by Alison Worthington

Originated by Grasmere Digital Imaging, Leeds, UK
Printed in China through World Print Ltd.

03 04 05 06   10 9 8 7 6 5 4 3 2 1

For a catalogue of all books published by Osprey Military and Aviation please contact:

Osprey Direct UK, P.O. Box 140, Wellingborough, Northants, NN8 2FA, UK
E-mail: info@ospreydirect.co.uk

Osprey Direct USA, c/o MBI Publishing, P.O. Box 1, 729 Prospect Ave, Osceola, WI 54020, USA
E-mail: info@ospreydirectusa.com

www.ospreypublishing.com

Author's note

Unless otherwise specified, the photographs used in this work were provided by the U-Boot Archiv in Cuxhaven-Altenbruch and I would like to express my gratitude to the Director of the Archiv, Horst Bredow, for his permission to reproduce these photos. Whilst the U-Boot Archiv might to some seem an unlikely source of photos of surface ships, it should be remembered that many U-boat men were former crewmembers of surface vessels and many of their personal photos have been donated to the Archiv. The Archiv also benefited from the donation of a huge number of photographic negatives from a former war correspondent, Walter Schöppe, including many photos of surface ships.

Artist's note

Readers may care to note that the original paintings from which the colour plates in this book were prepared are available for private sale. All reproduction copyright whatsoever is retained by the Publishers. All enquiries should be addressed to:

Ian Palmer, 15 Floriston Avenue, Hillingdon, Middlesex, UB10 9DZ, UK

The Publishers regret that they can enter into no correspondence upon this matter.

GERMAN HEAVY CRUISERS 1939-45

INTRODUCTION

In April 1919, the German government passed legislation governing the creation of a new navy, to be entitled the Reichsmarine, replacing the Imperial German Navy of the Kaiser's era. The High Seas Fleet had been ordered by the Allies to sail into the British base at Scapa Flow and there, after hearing the final terms of the Treaty of Versailles on 21 June, the German commanders had been ordered by Admiral Reuter to scuttle their vessels to prevent their subsequent use by the Allies. Enraged by the scuttling of the Fleet at Scapa Flow, the Allies simply seized most of the remaining German ships in reprisal, thus reducing the once powerful German fleet, boasting some of the most modern and powerful warships in existence, to a motley collection of light cruisers and obsolete pre-dreadnoughts.

The *Namensgeber* after whom the heavy cruisers were named. Left to right, Admiral Franz von Hipper, Blücher von Wahlstatt, Prince Eugene of Savoy. Below are original examples of the cap ribbons produced for these ships. (Author's collection)

Kreuzer Admiral Hipper

Kreuzer Prinz Eugen

Kreuzer Blücher

The Treaty of Versailles, signed by Germany on 28 June 1919, severely restricted the size and number of warships permitted to Germany.

Germany was restricted to six old pre-dreadnought battleships, six light cruisers, 12 destroyers and 12 torpedo boats. No submarines were permitted. Naval manpower was to be restricted to a total of 15,000, of which only 1,500 were to be of officer rank. The Armed Forces Law, passed by the Reichstag on 21 March 1921, stipulated that a further two pre-dreadnought battleships and two light cruisers could be held in reserve.

The terms of the Treaty of Versailles specified that these ships could not be replaced, let alone added to, until they were at least 20 years old. By 1923, however, only two battleships, the *Hannover* and *Braunschweig*, were in service, together with five cruisers and a number of torpedo boats. Faced with restraints on manpower and in warship construction, as well as a devastating economic burden of crippling reparation payments to her former enemies, the outlook for the German navy was bleak. Germany, however, having lost her best and most modern warships, was now in the position of being able to rebuild her fleet with brand new vessels, making use of the most up-to-date technology. Thus, although small in size, the Reichsmarine would possess some of the world's most modern warships at the beginning of the Second World War.

By 1925, the 'K' class of modern light cruisers (the *Königsberg*, *Köln* and *Karlsruhe*) had been added to the fleet, joined in 1927 by the *Leipzig*. By this point, however, there were still no new heavy units under construction. The terms of the Washington Agreement of February 1922 had laid restrictions on warship construction in an attempt to prevent an arms race. Although all of the major powers had signed, Germany had not been invited to attend. It was clear, however, that she would be held to the same terms.

The Agreement classified ships into two categories: capital ships with guns greater than 20cm calibre, and smaller ships with guns of a

Gebirgsjäger being transported to Norway during Operation Weserübung relax on the forecastle of *Admiral Hipper*. The mountain troops are dwarfed by the turrets of *Admiral Hipper*'s 20.3cm main armament.

Admiral Hipper in heavy seas. Visible at the bottom of this shot are the twin barrels of the 10.5cm heavy flak guns, fitted to triaxially-stabilised mounts.

lesser calibre and a maximum displacement of 11,900 metric tonnes (10,000 Imperial tons). This latter category was one that the Germans saw as providing them with the opportunity to create new and relatively powerful warships. German ingenuity was to create a hybrid formula from these restrictions, a vessel meeting the displacement limits set by the Agreement (effectively a large cruiser), but mounting guns of the calibre of a capital ship, the *Panzerschiffe* (pocket battleship).

A further treaty, the London Naval Agreement of April 1930, divided the cruiser class into two types, the heavy cruiser and the light cruiser. As both types were to be restricted to the 10,000-ton limit already mentioned, the classification clearly referred to the armament rather than the displacement of these vessels. The light cruiser would be permitted main armament of up to 15.5cm calibre (6.1 inches) and the heavy cruiser up to 20.3cm (8 inches). Existing laws, however, still set the maximum level of cruiser strength of the Reichsmarine at six light cruisers, no provision being made for the heavier type.

It was not until the conclusion of the Anglo-German Naval Treaty of June 1935 that such restrictions were set aside, with new restrictions simply setting the German navy's total strength at 35 per cent of that of the Royal Navy, but no longer with any restriction on the numbers of individual warship types. The Treaty effectively left Germany able to plan for the construction of five heavy cruisers, totalling just over 50,000 tons, within the terms of the London Naval Agreement. Shortly thereafter, the keel of the first unit, eventually to be known as the *Admiral Hipper*, was laid down at Hamberg.

THE HEAVY CRUISER

Firepower

The 20.3cm calibre gun mounted on the *Admiral Hipper* class was the largest permitted by the Treaty. The guns were mounted in four twin turrets, in the conventional layout of two forward and two aft. In German terminology, turrets were identified by letters, from bow to stern, thus 'Anton', 'Bruno', 'Caesar' and 'Dora'.

The 20.3cm gun had a muzzle velocity of 925m per second and fired a 122-kilo shell for a range, depending on trajectory, of up to 30,000m. Each barrel, including its breech mechanism, weighed around

21 tons. It was a quick-firing weapon, capable of a maximum theoretical rate of fire of four rounds per minute, an excellent rate of fire for heavy projectiles. There were three different types of projectile for these weapons: an armour-piercing shot containing 2.3 kilos of TNT, and two high explosive types, one with an 8.9-kilo TNT charge and the other with a smaller 6.5-kilo charge. Barrel life was estimated at around 600 rounds, after which it would need to be replaced. An equal mix of the three types of shell was to be carried, totalling some 960 rounds in all. However, in wartime, the total ammunition supply for the main armament could exceed 1,400 rounds.

The 10.5cm flak gun

The 10.5cm twin flak mounts on the heavy cruisers were of the same type installed on the *Bismarck* and *Scharnhorst* classes of battleships and the *Deutschland*-class pocket battleships, and featured triaxially-stabilised carriages. They fired with a muzzle velocity of 900m per second, discharging a 15.1-kilo projectile for a range of up to 17,700m against surface targets and 12,500m against aerial targets. Barrel life was around 2,950 rounds, and approximately 6,500 rounds of 10.5cm ammunition were carried, including about 240 rounds of tracer.

The 3.7cm flak gun

The secondary flak armament on the heavy cruisers, as on most large German warships, was the 3.7cm twin flak gun. This weapon fired a 0.74-kilo projectile at a muzzle velocity of 1,000m per second and had a range of around 8,500m against surface targets and 6,800m against aerial targets. Barrel life was around 7,500 rounds. Practical rate of fire was around 80 rounds per minute though as much as double this was possible in theory. The total number of 3.7cm guns carried could and did vary during wartime, and around 4,000 rounds of ammunition per barrel were carried.

The 2cm flak gun

This prolifically produced weapon was installed on all types of vessel, from U-boats to battleships. They were used in single, twin and quadruple configuration. The 2cm flak gun fired a 39.5-gr projectile with a muzzle velocity of 835m per second with a range from 4,900m against surface targets to 3,700m against aerial targets. A maximum rate of fire of up to 280 rounds per minute per barrel was theoretically possible, but around 120 rounds per minute was usual. This meant that the four-barrelled *Flakvierling* would put up at least 480 rounds per minute and usually nearer to 800, and with several such weapons in place a substantial hail of fire could be put up against low-flying aircraft that came too close. Approximately 3,000 rounds of 2cm ammunition were carried for each barrel.

Towards the end of the war, flak armament on most German warships was considerably enhanced. In addition, a limited number of 4cm Bofors flak guns were also installed on German

Flak gunners on *Admiral Hipper*. The combination of warm clothing and sun goggles being worn suggesting a bright winter's morning. Note the Kapok-filled life vests draped over the rail.

One of the triple torpedo tube sets on *Prinz Eugen*. Note the enclosed housing for the crew. The ship's Arado floatplane is taxiing alongside, about to be hoisted on board by the ship's crane.

vessels (again ranging from small E-boats up to capital ships) in the latter stages of the war. *Prinz Eugen* is known to have had a number of these fitted. These fired a 0.96-kilo projectile with a muzzle velocity of 854m per second and had a range of up to 7,000m.

Torpedoes

The heavy cruisers each carried four triple torpedo tube rotating mounts, two to port and two to starboard. The torpedoes carried were the G7a type, 53.3cm in diameter and weighing just over 1.5 tons. They were capable of speeds up to 44 knots. Twelve torpedoes were carried loaded in the tubes, with a further twelve stored.

Radar

The German navy played a leading role in the development of military radar systems. The Nachrichten Versuchsabteilung (NSV) had begun work on the development of sonar-type systems capable of detecting underwater targets as early as 1929. Using similar principles for operating above the surface, a rather primitive system was developed in 1933 that could pick up echoes using 13.5cm short-wave transmissions. In 1934, a new organisation, the Gesellschaft für Elektroakustische und Mechanische Apparate (GEMA) was founded to continue development in this area. The two organisations then strove to outdo each other in the attempt to produce an effective radio detection apparatus. By September 1935, a 48cm wavelength (630 MHz) set was tested before the CinC Navy, Admiral Raeder, and produced positive results using the training ship *Bremse* as a target (admittedly a rather large one).

The set was then installed for a time on the *Welle*, this small and rather unimposing vessel becoming the first German navy ship to carry functioning radar equipment. The set was tweaked somewhat to improve efficiency, settling on a wavelength of 82cm (368 MHz), which became the standard for all naval radar sets. German naval radar sets produced during this period and through to 1945 were predominantly developed by GEMA along with well-known firms such as Telefunken, Siemens, Lorenz and AEG.

German naval radar used a bewildering range of designations. In some cases this was deliberate and intended to confuse enemy intelligence. Early sets, for example, were referred to as DeTe (Dezimeter-Telegraphie) in an effort to disguise the true intent of the equipment.

Early operational radar sets were referred to as FMG (Funkmess-Gerät), or radar equipment, with suffixes indicating the year of manufacture, manufacturing company, frequency code letter and location on board ship. Thus, the set FMG 39G (gO), first installed on the *Admiral Graf Spee*, indicated: FMG – Fumkmess-Gerät; 39 – 1939; G – GEMA; g – code for 335 to 430 MHz; and O indicating its position as being mounted on the foretop rangefinder.

To confuse matters further, as radar developed, even more classification terminology was introduced,

including names as well as numbers. The FuSE 80 *Freya*, for instance, indicated: Fu – Funkmess or radar; S – Siemens, the manufacturer; E – Erkennung, search or reconnaissance radar; 80 – the development number; and *Freya* – the code name.

Fortunately, in 1943, a new, simplified designation system was introduced, in which the sets employed by the navy bore the designations FuMO (Funkmess-Ortung) active search radar, or FuMB (Funkmess-Beobachtung) passive detecting radar. This was then followed by a specific numerical code. The predominant types used on the heavy cruisers were the FuMO 25, FuMO 26, FuMO 27 and FuMB 4.

Fire control
Turret 'Anton'
The forward main turret of each ship was controlled by a 7m optical rangefinder unit mounted in an electrically powered rotating housing on the ship's foretop. In addition, a further 6m rangefinder was

A detail-filled view from the *Admiral Hipper* bridge area looking towards the stern. Note the lack of a funnel cap, suggesting an early date. Clearly seen are the aircraft catapult just in front of the mainmast, at bottom left the twin 10.5cm flak guns and one of the ship's boats. The spherical objects either side of the mainmast are the housings for the rangefinders controlling the heavy flak armament.

positioned in the forward fire control centre on the forward main superstructure just aft of turret 'Bruno'.

Turret 'Bruno'

The second turret could be controlled by either of the forward main fire control positions, but also had a built-in 7m rangefinder within the turret, the optics for which were contained within the projecting housing to the rear of the turret.

Turret 'Caesar'

The third main turret could be controlled by the aft main fire control position mounted on the roof of the aft control centre, but also had a built-in 7m rangefinder within the turret.

Turret 'Dora'

The fourth and aftmost main armament turret was controlled by the aft main fire control position. Like turret 'Anton', it had no built-in rangefinder of its own.

Flak

Main fire control for the heavy 10.5cm twin flak guns was provided by four 4m rangefinders, two in spherical housings to either side of the bridge and two in similar housings either side of the mainmast. These fed data down to battle control positions below decks.

SCHWERE KREUZER ADMIRAL HIPPER

The name

This, the first of Germany's new and powerful heavy cruisers, was named for Admiral Franz Ritter von Hipper (1863–1932). Hipper had joined the Imperial German Navy in April 1881 and was commissioned as a Leutnant zur See in 1884. He progressed gradually through the ranks, gaining considerable experience on various types and sizes of warship until reaching the rank of Konteradmiral in December 1912. He commanded the German battlecruiser fleet with considerable skill, in particular during the Battle of Jutland in 1916. His successes brought him promotion to Vizeadmiral and a knighthood from the Kingdom of Bavaria. By 1918 he had reached the rank of full Admiral and eventually commanded the entire fleet. He survived the war and died in retirement at the age of 68 on 25 May 1932.

Armorial crest

Prior to the outbreak of war, when all such crests were removed, *Admiral Hipper* bore the crest of the Hipper family, a shield bearing a central vertical staff superimposed over three crowns.

An Arado 196 floatplane being hoisted aboard *Prinz Eugen*. Its wings are folded, ready for stowage in the ship's hangar.

ADMIRAL HIPPER SPECIFICATIONS

Length	202.8m
Beam	21.3m
Draught	7.74m
Maximum displacement	18,600 tons
Fuel oil carried	3,050 tons
Maximum speed	32 knots
Endurance	6,800 nautical miles
Main armament	8 x 20.3cm guns in four twin turrets
Secondary armament	12 x 10.5cm guns in six twin turrets
Flak armament	12 x 3.7cm guns in six twin turrets
	8 x 2cm guns on single mounts
Torpedoes	12 x 53.3cm torpedo tubes in four triple mounts
Aircraft	3 x Arado 196 floatplanes
Complement	50 officers and 1,500 men

Ship's commanders

Kapitän zur See Hellmuth Heye	April 1939–September 1940
Kapitän zur See Wilhelm Meisel	September 1940–November 1942
Kapitän zur See Hans Hartmann	November 1942–February 1943
Kapitän zur See Hans Henigst	March 1944–May 1945

General construction data

Admiral Hipper was protected by a partially armoured main deck, ranging from 12mm to 25mm in thickness. The armoured deck, one deck below, was some 30mm thick. The main belt of the hull, referred to as the 'citadel', had side armour 80mm thick, reducing to 40mm towards the bow and 70mm towards the stern. The turrets for the main armament had 70mm thick walls, with frontal armour 160mm thick, and a rear wall 90mm thick on turrets 'Anton' and 'Dora' and 60mm thick on 'Bruno' and 'Caesar'.

Modifications

As first completed, *Admiral Hipper* featured a straight stem and an

A three-quarter bow view of *Admiral Hipper* in the early part of her career. Note the crewman in whites standing on the boat boom to which one of the ship's cutters is tethered.

uncapped funnel. Her armorial crest was fitted to the stem. In November 1939, she underwent a refit in which her straight stem was replaced by a 'clipper bow' and her funnel had a raked cap fitted. At the same time, her armorial crests changed from a single piece on the stem, to one each side of the bow. In reality, however, it seems that only the mounting points for these shields were fitted. After the outbreak of war, such devices were removed from all warships or painted over.

Subsequent to the outbreak of war, the only significant modifications made to *Admiral Hipper* were in terms of increases to her anti-aircraft protection. Quadruple 2cm flak mounts were added to the roof of turret 'Bruno' and turret 'Caesar' in 1942, though by the end of the war these had been replaced by 4cm Bofors-type single-barrelled weapons.

Powerplant

Admiral Hipper was driven by three Blohm & Voss steam turbine engines, one mounted on the ship's centre line and one each to port and starboard. The aftmost (central) engine was located in line with the aft control centre whilst the port and starboard engines were just forward of the line of the mainmast. Each of the three propeller shafts was fitted with a three-blade propeller some 4m in diameter. A single centrally mounted rudder was fitted and was electrically steered.

A total of 12 LaMont-type boilers were installed on *Admiral Hipper*, two to port and two to starboard in each of three boiler rooms situated from a point just ahead of the engine room for the central engine, and reaching to a point in line with the rear of the forward control centre. These produced a working pressure of 85 atmospheres.

In addition, *Admiral Hipper* was provided with four 150kW diesel generators, four 460kW turbo generators and two 230kW turbo generators to provide for her considerable demand for electrical power, and having the capacity to produce almost 3,000kW of electrical output.

Radar

No radar was installed on *Admiral Hipper* as first built, but in late 1940 FuMO 22 surface search radar was installed and in 1941/42 FuMO 27 sets with a 3m x 4m 'mattress' antenna were mounted on the fire control stations on the foretop and on the aft fire control centre. In the latter part of the war, the fittings for an additional FuMO 25 with 3m x 2m antenna were installed, but it is unclear whether this equipment was actually fitted.

Colour scheme and camouflage

As first completed, *Admiral Hipper* sported the usual pale grey colour scheme used on most German warships of that period. The maindeck level was covered by wooden planking and most other horizontal surfaces by an anti-slip material in dark grey colour. A large white circle containing a black swastika was painted on the forecastle to assist in aerial recognition. In early 1940, the roofs of the main armament turrets were painted yellow. In the spring of 1940, *Admiral Hipper* was given a disruptive camouflage paint scheme consisting of angular 'splinter' pattern patches of dark grey over the pale grey base coat. Although the exact pattern changed on at least two subsequent occasions, in early 1942 and again in early 1944, the basic theme of a dark grey pattern over the lighter grey base remained throughout the remainder of the war.

Gebirgsjäger from the army about to embark on *Admiral Hipper* for transport to Norway. Note the additional flak armament fitted to the roof of turret 'Bruno'. (Naval Historical Collection)

Pre-war service

The *Admiral Hipper* was laid down at the Blohm & Voss yard in Hamburg on 6 July 1935, some eight months after the contract for her manufacture was placed. Construction of the basic hull and super-structure took 19 months, the ship finally being launched on 6 February 1937. The launch ceremony was carried out by Frau Raeder, the wife of the Commander in Chief Navy, Grossadmiral Raeder. A further two years were taken to fit her out and she was finally commissioned into the Kriegsmarine, the first of her class, on 29 April 1939 after completing her trials.

The ship then spent the next few weeks working up in Baltic waters, and taking the opportunity to make courtesy calls in Estonian and Swedish ports. During August, live firing trials were carried out in the Baltic. *Admiral Hipper* was still working up when war broke out and, although she was briefly used in patrol activities, she did not see combat and returned to her gunnery trials shortly thereafter. On completion of these trials she returned to Hamburg and the Blohm & Voss yards. Final fitting out work was done, and at the same time her original straight stem was replaced with a so-called 'Atlantic' clipper bow, and her funnel given a raked cap.

Admiral Hipper during fitting out. The main armament turrets have been installed but little work has been done on the superstructure.

Wartime service

On completion of the modifications, *Admiral Hipper* returned to her Baltic trials in January 1940 but was forced back to port, putting into Wilhelmshaven because of severe icing. On 17 February, she was pronounced operational and on the following day set off on her first war patrol. In consort with the battlecruisers *Gneisenau* and *Scharnhorst* she searched for British merchant shipping in the waters off Bergen, but to no avail, and was back in port just two days later.

Admiral Hipper's next mission was to transport troops committed to Operation Weserübung, the invasion of Norway. A number of the Army's elite Gebirgstruppen were taken on board at Cuxhaven from whence they were to be taken to Trondheim, the port to be secured by a task force consisting of *Admiral Hipper* supported by four destroyers.

En route, the German force received an order that the *Admiral Hipper* should detach itself and proceed to search for the destroyer *Bernd von Arnim*, which had reported exchanging fire with a British warship. Minutes later, *Admiral Hipper* encountered the British destroyer *Glowworm*. The British destroyer mis-identified the German heavy cruiser as a 'friendly', and so it was *Admiral Hipper* who had the advantage of opening fire first. Hits were soon scored on the smaller British warship as the German rapidly closed with her. Soon the two ships were so close that *Admiral Hipper* could no longer depress her main armament far enough to engage *Glowworm*. The cruiser's 10.5cm heavy flak guns, however, delivered a hail of fire on the enemy. The German suffered one significant hit on the starboard bow, but the British warship was devastated by the weight of fire it received from *Admiral Hipper*. The latter was constantly manoeuvring to present as small a target as possible to the destroyer, fearing the *Glowworm* would launch torpedoes. This, in fact, she did but unfortunately for the British all missed the target. Unbeknown to the Germans, *Glowworm* had suffered rudder failure that, fortuitously for the British in view of the close range, had put her on a collision course with *Admiral Hipper*. The latter had no time to manoeuvre out of danger and was hit by *Glowworm* on her starboard side some way back from the bow. Shortly after the collision, the destroyer's boilers exploded, sending the warship to the bottom in only a matter of seconds. Forty survivors were rescued by the German cruiser.

Admiral Hipper then continued on her voyage towards Trondheim. She succeeded in passing the Norwegian defences on the approaches to the port by identifying herself as a British warship when challenged. The time gained by this ruse meant that by the time the Norwegians opened fire, *Admiral Hipper* was able to speed past them before any damage could be done, with smoke and dust thrown up by answering fire from *Admiral Hipper* helping to obscure the vision of the defenders. *Admiral Hipper* docked safely at Trondheim just before 0530hrs on 9 April 1940 and disembarked her passengers.

Once the nearby Norwegian coastal artillery positions had fallen into German hands, making it safe for her to leave Trondheim, *Admiral Hipper* set sail for home once again. She was escorted part of the way by the destroyer *Friedrich Eckoldt* which, after being released, came under attack from Allied aircraft out hunting the *Admiral Hipper*, but fortunately survived. The heavy cruiser reached Wilhelmshaven safely on 12 April.

Taken into dry dock, it was discovered that the damage to *Admiral Hipper* was more extensive that had been first thought, but nevertheless within two weeks all the necessary repairs had been made and she was once again fit for sea. In June, the heavy cruiser was tasked with joining the battleships *Scharnhorst* and *Gneisenau*, supported by four destroyers, and capturing the port of Harstad from the Anglo-French forces in occupation. En route to their target, however, the Germans learned that the Allies had already abandoned the port, and the warships were given an alternative mission – to hunt down an Allied convoy reported in the vicinity.

On 9 June, *Admiral Hipper* and *Gneisenau* encountered a British tanker escorted by a naval trawler. *Gneisenau* dispatched the tanker whilst *Admiral Hipper* took care of the escort, a rather uneven match. Shortly afterwards, *Hipper* intercepted and sank the 20,000-ton troop carrier *Orama* before returning to Trondheim once again to refuel.

A period of relative quiet followed, though *Admiral Hipper*'s flak gunners succeeded in shooting down a British bomber on 13 June. On

A further view of *Admiral Hipper*'s forward superstructure, during the embarkation of her passengers. Clearly shown here is the searchlight platform just above the enclosed bridge and the heavy flak guns pointing skywards with their spherical fire control housing just above.

25 July, while on contraband patrol, *Admiral Hipper* intercepted the Finnish freighter *Ester Thorden*, only to find that as well as the stated cargo of timber destined for the United States, she carried over 1.75 tons of gold. Rather than sinking her, the Germans sent her into an occupied Norwegian port under a prize crew.

In September 1940, *Admiral Hipper* returned to Wilhelmshaven for an overhaul. Towards the end of that month the cruiser sailed on a mission intended to see her break out into the Atlantic on a raiding mission. She sustained severe damage to the engine oil feed that resulted in a serious fire. For several hours, the cruiser drifted helplessly as engines were shut down so that the blaze could be tackled. Fortunately, there was no contact with the enemy during these dangerous hours and, the blaze eventually extinguished, on 30 September she limped back into Hamburg and spent just over a week undergoing repairs at the Blohm & Voss yard.

On 30 November, she sailed once again on her mission to attack Allied merchantmen in the Atlantic, successfully passing undetected through the Denmark Strait on 6 December. On 24 December, *Admiral Hipper* intercepted an Allied convoy consisting of around 20 troopships and covered by a sizeable escort consisting of a heavy cruiser, two light cruisers, an aircraft carrier and six destroyers. The powerful escort, however, was not immediately detected by the Germans. *Admiral Hipper* opened fire on two merchantmen, which suffered considerable damage from her main armament. At this point, however, the heavy cruiser and destroyer escorts were spotted and the German withdrew under covering fire from her main armament, fearing a torpedo attack from the enemy destroyers.

Around ten minutes later, the enemy cruiser was spotted again off *Admiral Hipper*'s port bow and the German opened fire, scoring hits near the British warship's aft turrets, on her waterline and also on her forward superstructure. At this point, *Admiral Hipper* disengaged, mindful of the torpedo danger presented by the enemy cruiser's destroyer escort screen. During the engagement, in which the *Admiral Hipper* had damaged two merchantmen and engaged and damaged an enemy warship, part of a much more powerful force, she herself had suffered no damage. Now running short of fuel, *Admiral Hipper* set sail for friendly territory and docked in Brest on 27 December.

A snapshot of *Admiral Hipper* taken from a U-boat whilst on training exercises in the Baltic. This shot gives a good view of her midships section. Note the flak gun platform fitted on the roof of turret 'Caesar' and the extensive modification to the rangefinder housing on the foretop when compared with earlier photographs.

After undergoing minor repairs in the French port, *Admiral Hipper* sailed again on 1 February 1941. It had originally been intended that *Admiral Hipper* would operate in a battlegroup with the *Scharnhorst* and *Gneisenau,* with the cruiser to act as a diversion to draw British warships away from the areas in which the battleships would operate. This plan was abandoned when *Gneisenau* suffered storm damage at the end of December and was forced to return to Germany for repairs. *Admiral Hipper* therefore departed for her new mission alone.

After refuelling from a German tanker near the Azores, the cruiser headed eastwards, and on 11 February she intercepted and sank a lone British freighter. Later that day, however, she made radar contact with a British convoy, SL 64, which comprised 19 ships and which she shadowed until the following morning. Drawing near to the convoy, *Admiral Hipper* successfully passed herself off as a British warship until she was close enough to attack. Drawing alongside, she struck the British flag she was flying and, running up the German war flag, opened fire on the nearest merchantmen. For the next half-hour or so, the German cruiser prowled back and forth along the length of the convoy's outermost column, firing with main armament, heavy flak guns and torpedoes. Having decimated this outer column, *Admiral Hipper* sped off after the remainder of the convoy and turned her fire on the surviving luckless merchant ships. When *Admiral Hipper* finally broke away, fearing the arrival of British warships, a total of 13 merchant ships had been claimed sunk by the Germans. British authorities insisted only seven ships had been sunk and two damaged, but as some convoy survivors actually claimed that 14 ships had been sunk, it does seem that the British figures may be too low.

Admiral Hipper, now running low on fuel and ammunition, set sail for Brest, arriving on 15 February to a rapturous welcome. Brest, however, was receiving too much attention from British bombers and the decision was taken to move *Admiral Hipper* back to Germany. On 15 March, after undergoing repairs to damage caused by underwater wreckage in the harbour as she docked, the cruiser set sail once again. She successfully negotiated the Denmark Strait and, after a call at Bergen to refuel, reached Kiel on 28 March. Taken into the Deutsche Werke yard, she underwent a major overhaul and refit, being out of service for some seven months before returning to the safer waters of the Baltic for trials. After 21 December, she put into Gotenhafen for further minor refit work.

January 1942 saw even more overhaul work being performed, this time on her turbines at the Blohm & Voss yards in Hamburg, during

Admiral Hipper sporting one of several splinter-style disruptive camouflage schemes used in the second half of the war. This consisted of a dark grey pattern over the standard pale grey base coat. The FuMO radar antenna can just be discerned on the enlarged foretop rangefinder housing.

which time a degaussing coil was also fitted to her hull. In March, *Admiral Hipper*, in consort with a number of destroyers and torpedo boats, moved to Trondheim to join *Admiral Scheer* and *Prinz Eugen*, though the latter returned to Germany for repairs in mid-May.

On 3 July, *Admiral Hipper*, with *Tirpitz*, *Lützow* and *Admiral Scheer*, was tasked with attacking the large British convoy PQ17, en route to Murmansk. The operation, known as Rösselsprung, was a disaster. *Lützow*, along with two of the escorting destroyers, ran aground. The remaining warships continued on, but the British had become aware of their presence and had ordered the convoy to scatter. Once the Germans learned of this, they realised the futility of sending a small but powerful group of warships to search for a widely dispersed convoy and ordered the warships to return to their anchorages. The attack on the convoy, however, continued but was carried out by U-boats and Luftwaffe aircraft. A total of 21 ships were sunk in one of Britain's worst naval disasters.

Admiral Hipper had a fairly uneventful time over the next two months, though she did escape an attempt at torpedoing by the British submarine *Tigris* on 10 September whilst on patrol with *Admiral Scheer* and the cruiser *Köln*. In late September, she did, however, take part in a successful minelaying operation, the purpose of which was to lay minefields which would force enemy ships to sail closer to the Norwegian coast, and within easy reach of German warships, in order to avoid the mines. Most of the month of October was spent in Bogen Bay near Narvik, where she underwent engine repairs.

The *Admiral Hipper* saw action again in the closing hours of the year, putting to sea along with the *Lützow* and an escorting force of destroyers in an attempt to intercept and destroy a British convoy, JW 51B, which had been detected by a U-boat whilst on its way to Murmansk. On 31 December 1942, at around 0720hrs, the German force made contact with the convoy. *Admiral Hipper*, designated flagship and under the command of Admiral Kummetz, and the destroyers *Friedrich Eckoldt*, *Richard Beitzen* and Z 24, were to the north of the convoy, faced by an escort of five British destroyers. *Lützow* and her three destroyer escorts lay further to the south, and raced northwards at best speed when informed of contact being made with the enemy. At

A fine view of *Admiral Hipper's* spacious quarterdeck. Here the crew would muster on ceremonial occasions to be addressed by the commanding officer.

around 0930hrs, German destroyers opened fire on the British escorts, but without scoring any hits. Ten minutes later, *Admiral Hipper* engaged with her main and heavy flak armament, again without scoring any significant hits. For the next two hours, the smallest and most weakly armed of the British destroyers, *Obedient* and *Obdurate*, with only 4-inch guns as their main armament, shepherded their merchant charges, protecting them against attack from the German destroyers whilst the three larger escorts, *Achates*,

A shot of *Admiral Hipper*'s stern, showing to good advantage the anchor in its shaped hull recess. Prior to the outbreak of war, a large cast bronze national emblem (eagle clutching a swastika) was mounted on the stern.

Onslow and *Orwell*, fended off the German cruiser. Although outgunned, the smaller British ships made difficult targets and the potential of their torpedo armament posed a constant threat to the cruiser. The heavy firepower of *Admiral Hipper*'s 20.3cm guns was too much for the enemy destroyers, however, and at around 1018hrs, a number of direct hits on *Onslow* left her burning fiercely. Shortly thereafter, *Admiral Hipper* ran into the diminutive minesweeper *Bramble*, which she quickly engaged and reduced to a blazing hulk. As the cruiser moved southwards in pursuit of the convoy, it was left to two of the German destroyers, *Friedrich Eckoldt* and *Richard Beitzen*, to sink the unfortunate *Bramble*.

Unbeknown to the Germans, however, two British cruisers, the *Sheffield* and the *Jamaica*, were rapidly approaching from the north, their approach shielded by the appalling weather, replete with snow squalls.

Meanwhile *Admiral Hipper* had caught up with the destroyer *Achates*, pulverising her with numerous direct hits from her 20.3cm main armament. *Achates* was left a blazing wreck. The three remaining British destroyers now turned away from the convoy to offer assistance to *Achates*. Forced to turn away to the north to avoid the threat of torpedoes from the enemy destroyers, *Admiral Hipper* sailed directly into the path of *Jamaica* and *Sheffield* and came under heavy fire. Heeling over as she turned sharply to port, her thinly armoured lower hull was exposed and she took a direct hit from a British shell, which penetrated below the waterline and exploded in her engine room causing extensive flooding. A mixture of having been taken by surprise, severe icing of her rangefinder equipment, and smoke from the onboard fires caused by several direct hits from enemy 6-inch shells all conspired to prevent *Admiral Hipper* from loosing off more than a few ineffectual salvos at the British warships as she retired westwards at speed, away from the enemy. In view of the serious damage to *Admiral Hipper*, Kummetz ordered the action broken off, as his orders were not to risk his ship.

In this atmospheric shot taken from the deck of the battleship *Tirpitz*, the German squadron sorties out from its Norwegian anchorage. *Tirpitz* leads, with *Admiral Hipper* following and with an escort of two destroyers on the flank. *Admiral Hipper* can be seen to be sporting one of her disruptive camouflage patterns.

Blücher during trials. The need for the funnel cap later fitted is clearly illustrated here. The volumes of smoke issuing from the funnel could at times obscure vision from the foretop optical rangefinder.

Even more unfortunate were the destroyers *Richard Beitzen* and *Friedrich Eckoldt*, which now strayed into the path of the British cruisers. A fatal error in identification led to *Friedrich Eckoldt* believing that the British cruisers were in fact German ships, and by the time she realised her error it was too late. She was annihilated by the overwhelming firepower of the enemy ships at virtually point-blank range, and blew up and sank with all hands.

Lützow had closed with the convoy by then, but was suffering the same problems with icing to her rangefinder equipment that had dogged *Admiral Hipper*. She opened fire briefly on the convoy but did no significant damage before being ordered by the flagship to break off the action and return to base. The German force returned to its anchorage in Alta Fjord on 1 January 1943.

Recriminations, with far-reaching consequences, began almost immediately. Unfortunately, a signal from a U-boat attempting to monitor the action was misinterpreted, and high command were led to believe that a victory had been gained. As the truth began to unfold, it was realised that a destroyer had been lost and the *Admiral Hipper* crippled, but no single enemy merchantman had been sunk. To cap the German misery, British accounts of the action bragged of having seen off a German force much more powerful than the escorting vessels (*Admiral Hipper* with 8-inch and *Lützow* with 11-inch guns opposing

Blücher during fitting out. Note that the straight stem has already been replaced by the clipper-style 'Atlantic' bow. All four main armament turrets have been installed and work on the main superstructure is at an advanced stage.

two British cruisers with 6-inch guns, and six German destroyers facing just five British ones). Hitler flew into a towering rage, insisting that the navy was useless and ordered that all its heavy units be scrapped and their guns transferred for use on land. The protests of the CinC navy, Grossadmiral Raeder, were to no avail, and growing animosity between Raeder and Hitler led the former to offer his resignation, which Hitler accepted. His successor was the CinC U-boats, Karl Dönitz. Thankfully for the navy, the new Grossadmiral did manage to tone down Hitler's orders somewhat, and the scrapping order was rescinded, though several warships were to be taken out of active service. Hitler, however, never again put his faith in the heavy units of the Kriegsmarine.

On her return to Alta Fjord, emergency repairs were carried out on *Admiral Hipper* allowing her to proceed safely to Bogen Bay in late January 1943. Remaining there for two weeks, she departed on 7 February with the cruiser *Köln* and a destroyer escort, eventually making her way, via Trondheim and Kiel, to Wilhelmshaven. There, on 28 February, the once-proud cruiser was decommissioned, victim of Hitler's spite against the navy, though repair work on her continued. In April, still not fully repaired, *Admiral Hipper* was towed to the safer haven of Pillau on the Baltic.

Almost a year later, the *Admiral Hipper* was taken into Gotenhafen for repair work to be completed with the intent of placing her back into service for use in the Baltic. She was re-commissioned into the Kriegsmarine, though it was not intended to use her for active combat service, but as a cadet training vessel. In the event, for the next five months she carried out trials in the Baltic but was never able to reach operational status. She was, in any case, effectively taken out of use once again by virtue of her crew being virtually press-ganged into labouring on the digging of defensive ditches on the approaches to Gotenhafen as the Red Army drew ever nearer. Things were made worse by the Royal Air Force laying an extensive minefield in the waters around the port, effectively trapping the cruiser.

At the end of 1944, *Admiral Hipper* was once again scheduled for overhaul and repairs with the intent of bringing her up to standard for full operational duties. Work was scheduled to last for approximately three months, but at the end of January the situation on the Eastern Front had deteriorated so much that the ship, despite having only one operational engine, was ordered to sail for Germany. Sailing on 29 January, *Admiral Hipper* finally reached Kiel four days later. Here she was taken into the Germaniawerft yards where her refit and repairs were to continue.

Admiral Hipper's luck ran out on 3 May when she was hit in an RAF bombing raid and fatally damaged. She was scuttled at her moorings. The remains of the once magnificent warship were broken up for scrap in 1949.

SCHWERE KREUZER BLÜCHER

The name

The second of the Kriegsmarine's new heavy cruisers was named after one of Germany's greatest military heroes, Generalfeldmarschall Gebhard Leberecht Fürst Blücher von Wahlstatt. Blücher was a prickly character who had resigned his first commission in the Prussian Army after feeling slighted by being overlooked for promotion. After the death of the Prussian king, Frederick the Great, and the accession to the throne of Friedrich Wilhelm, Blücher rejoined the Prussian Army in 1787 and began to rise through the ranks. By 1801, he held the rank of Generalleutnant and had proven himself a skilled cavalryman. During the Napoleonic wars, Blücher at one time found himself a prisoner after his troops were forced to surrender once their supplies and ammunition were exhausted. Fortunately, he was included in an exchange of high-ranking prisoners, a practice not uncommon at that time, and was soon back in action. In June 1815, his timely arrival on the battlefield at Waterloo secured victory against Napoleon. So great was his contribution to the defeat of Napoleon that his grateful king created a unique grade of the Iron Cross for him, the Breast Star, thereafter known as the Blücher-stern, after its sole recipient. Blücher, much beloved by the men he commanded, died just a few months after his victory at Waterloo.

Blücher in her prime. Her funnel cap has now been fitted and the ship looks in pristine condition. Many of her crew are mustered on the forecastle.

Armorial crest

The crest mounted on the *Blücher* was the family crest of its illustrious namesake, consisting of a quartered shield with a crowned black Prussian eagle at top left and bottom right. At bottom left was the Iron Cross and at top right was a ring of laurel leaves with a superimposed sword sitting diagonally with its hilt at bottom right. Superimposed on the main shield was a small central shield bearing two black keys facing away from each other.

BLÜCHER SPECIFICATIONS

Length	202.8m
Beam	21.3m
Draught	7.74m
Maximum displacement	18,694 tons
Main armament	8 x 20.3cm guns in four twin turrets
Secondary armament	12 x 10.5cm guns in six twin turrets
Flak armament	12 x 3.7cm guns in six twin turrets
	8 x 2cm guns on single mounts
Torpedoes	12 x 53.3cm torpedo tubes in four triple mounts
Aircraft	3 x Arado 196 floatplanes
Complement	50 officers and 1,500 men

Ship's commanders

Kapitän zur See Heinrich Woldag   September 1939–April 1940

General construction data

The *Blücher* was laid down at the Blohm & Voss shipyard in Hamburg on 15 August 1936, just over a year after *Admiral Hipper* and some 20 months after the contract for her manufacture was placed. Construction of the basic hull and superstructure took just ten months, the ship being launched on 8 June 1937, four months after her sister. Armour protection for the *Blücher* was basically the same as for *Admiral Hipper*, as the two ships were nearly identical. Fitting out and finishing work took just over two years and she was finally commissioned into the Kriegsmarine on 20 September 1939.

This shot shows *Blücher* during pre-war trials. Note the heraldic shields, removed at the outbreak of war, are still carried on her bow. The clipper bow has been installed but the funnel still lacks the distinctive raked cap later fitted to all three of this class.

The final bow configuration for *Blücher* is shown here. Note the change in anchor positions from that shown in the photograph of her launch. There are now one to either side of the bow, in an anchor cluse on the forecastle, and one on the stem itself.

Modifications

As launched, like her older sister, *Blücher* featured a straight stem and uncapped funnel. Unlike her sister, *Blücher* did not have two bow anchors, one on each side located in an anchor cluse on the edge of the forecastle, but the earlier layout of two anchors to port and one to starboard, each emerging from an anchor port on the hullside. During her fitting out, however, and before she was commissioned into the navy, her configuration was altered to match that of *Admiral Hipper*, with one bow anchor either side of a raked clipper bow. A raked funnel cap was also added, but not until some time after the bow modifications, as original photos show her with the clipper bows, but still lacking the funnel cap.

Powerplant

Blücher, like her sister *Admiral Hipper*, was driven by three Blohm & Voss steam turbine engines, one mounted on the ship's centre line and one each to port and starboard. The aftmost (central) engine was located in line with the aft control centre whilst the port and starboard engines were just forward of the line of the mainmast. Each of the three propeller shafts was fitted with a three-blade propeller some 4m in diameter. A single centrally mounted rudder was fitted and was electrically steered.

A total of 12 Wagner-type boilers were installed on *Blücher*, two to port and two to starboard in each of three boiler rooms situated from a point just ahead of the engine room for the central engine, and reaching to a point in line with the rear of the forward control centre. These produced a working pressure of 85 atmospheres.

In addition, *Blücher* was provided with four 150kW diesel generators, four 460kW turbo generators and two 230kW turbo generators to provide for her considerable demand for electrical power, and having the capacity to produce almost 3,000kW of electrical output. This specification was exactly the same as on *Admiral Hipper*.

Radar

Due to her extremely brief life, *Blücher* did not see much in the way of radar modifications. She had an FuMO 22 with a 2m x 6m mattress antenna fitted to her foretop rangefinder housing. This was the only radar she was to carry.

Colour schemes and camouflage

Blücher was completed in the traditional pale grey livery of German warships of her period. Her short life came to an end before any of the more elaborate camouflage schemes were introduced.

Wartime service

Following her commissioning, *Blücher* spent the major part of

November 1939 receiving additional improvements in dock, but was eventually able to put to sea at the end of the month, sailing for Gotenhafen where she carried out trials until the middle of December. Thereafter, she returned to Kiel for final modifications to be made before returning to the Baltic at the beginning of January 1940 to continue working up to operational level. By mid-January she had returned to Keil once more and, due to extreme weather conditions, found herself iced in until the end of the month. At this stage she moved to the Deutsche Werke yard for yet more improvement work to be carried out, remaining there for two months.

Finally, on 5 April 1940, *Blücher* was considered ready for active duties, albeit a month or so before originally planned, and was allocated to the forces assigned to Operation Weserübung, the invasion of Norway. *Blücher* was to take part in the seizure of the port of Oslo, delivering a force of German army troops to seize the port.

That day, Konteradmiral Kummetz came onboard at Swinemünde, as did some 800 troops from 163 Infanterie Division with a full load of equipment and ammunition. Early on the morning of 8 April, *Blücher* set sail for Norwegian waters, accompanied by the pocket battleship *Lützow* and the light cruiser *Emden* and a number of smaller escorts. Passing through the Kattegat and Skagerrak, they were spotted by a British submarine, HMS *Triton*, which launched a torpedo at *Blücher*. Although this missed, the German force had been detected and was now on the alert for further enemy attacks.

Darkness had fallen as the Germans neared the approaches to Oslofjord. Just after midnight, the German ships were illuminated by searchlights from the Norwegian coastal artillery batteries on Bolarne and Ranoy islands, but no shots were fired. Shortly afterwards, however, as the German warships continued on their way towards Oslo, a warning shot rang out and the navigation lights at the mouth of the fjord were extinguished, making the passage in darkness that much more hazardous.

At 0046hrs, *Blücher* stopped and unloaded most of the German infantrymen she was carrying onto the smaller escorting ships before continuing northwards. At 0440hrs she was once again illuminated by Norwegian searchlights and at 0521hrs the heavy 28cm guns at Oskarsborg opened fire to her port side, scoring immediate and devastating hits at short range. The German vessels had been ordered not to open fire unless fired upon first but now could not pinpoint the exact location of the enemy guns on shore. *Blücher* was brought up to full speed in an attempt to rush past the enemy shore defences before too much damage could be done, but the 15cm guns

Blücher **running at full speed during her trials. Note the huge amount of black smoke belching from her funnel. Also clear in this photograph is the open bridge of her command tower.**

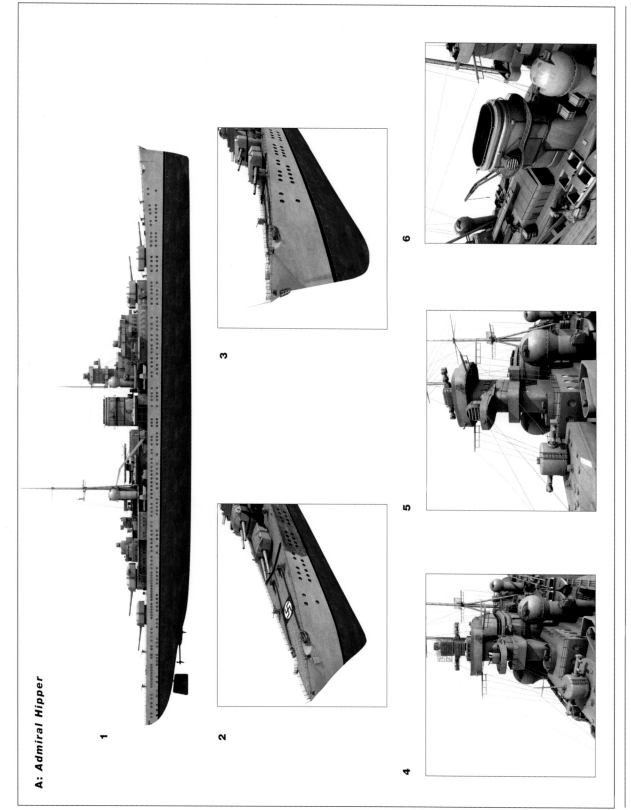

A: *Admiral Hipper*

1

2

3

4

5

6

B: *Admiral Hipper* in action

C: Blücher

1

2

3

4

5

C

D: *PRINZ EUGEN*

KEY

1 4cm flak gun
2 20.3cm turret 'Anton'
3 20.3cm turret 'Bruno'
4 4cm flak gun
5 Bridge
6 Flak platform
7 Forward main fire control director with 6m rangefinder
8 Foretop fire control director with 7m rangefinder
9 Foremast
10 Funnel
11 Mainmast
12 Searchlight
13 Radar antenna
14 Catapult
15 Aft flak fire control director
16 Aft fire control director with 7m rangefinder
17 3.3cm medium flak gun
18 20.3cm turret 'Caesar'

19 20.3cm turret 'Dora'
20 4cm flak gun
21 Aerial recognition flag
22 Rudder
23 Propeller
24 Engine room
25 Aft port torpedo tubes
26 Control room and damage control centre
27 10.5cm flak gun
28 Aircraft hanger
29 Ship's crane
30 Trunking to funnel
31 Launch
32 Boiler rooms
33 Forward port torpedo tubes
34 Turbo-generator room
35 10.5cm flak gun
36 Foreword flak fire control director
37 Shell hoist room
38 Powder hoist room

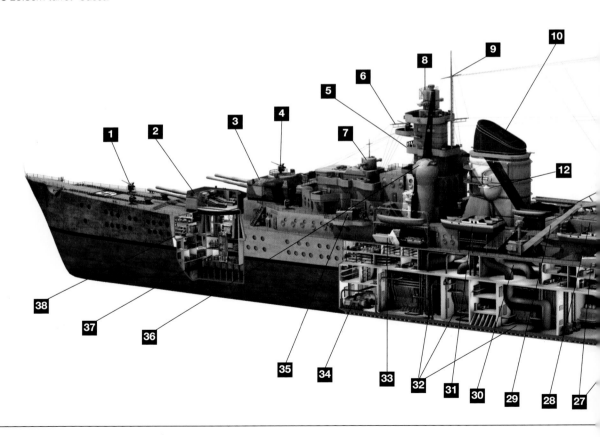

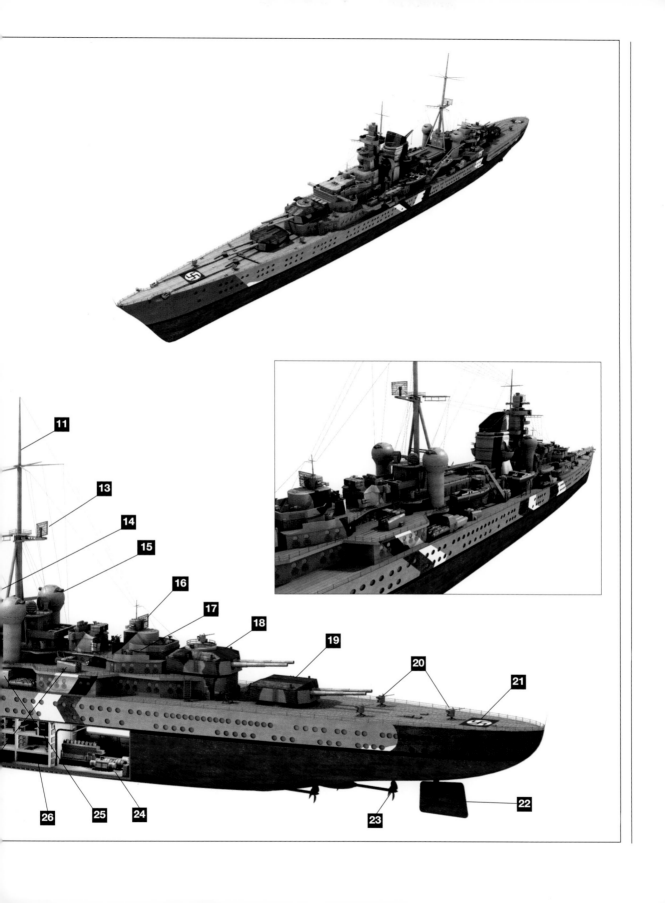

E: *Prinz Eugen*

1

2

3

4

E

F: *Prinz Eugen* in action

G: Late-war camouflage scheme

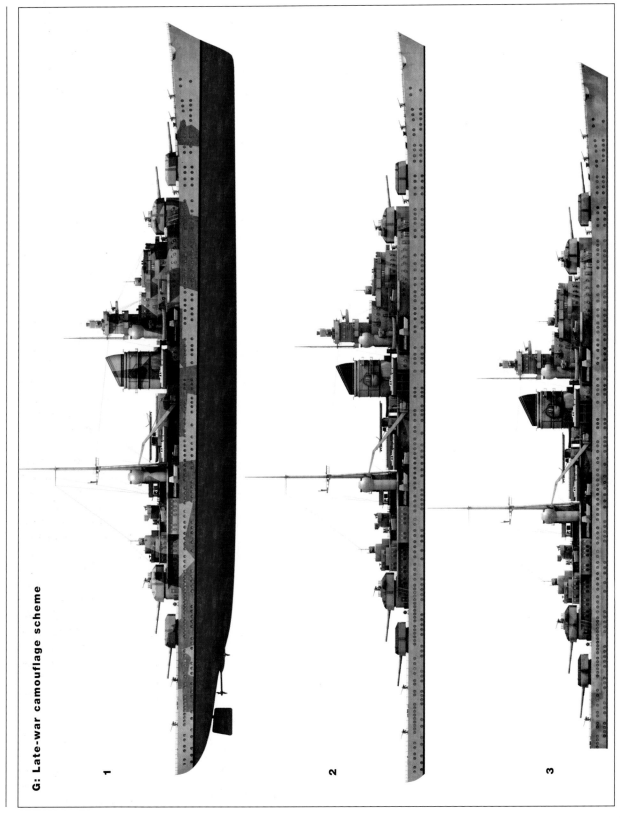

1

2

3

on Dobrak, on *Blücher*'s starboard side, now also opened fire at a range of just 400 yards, virtually point-blank range when shooting at such a large target. Disaster struck a few moments later when, at 0530hrs, *Blücher* was hit by two torpedoes.

By this time, the severely wounded cruiser had almost passed the danger point and the Norwegian guns were finding it impossible to traverse far enough to get her in their sights. Firing stopped at 0534hrs.

Lützow, seeing the devastation wrought upon her companion, hesitated to proceed and, in fact, her own forward turret was put out of action by a direct hit. She therefore reversed course, edging away from the danger point.

Looking from between the guns of turret 'Anton' towards *Blücher*'s bow. Note the large anchor capstans and the swastika symbol, a feature added to the forecastle of many of the larger German warships as an aid to aerial recognition.

Blücher at sea during training exercises, photographed from the deck of a passing E-boat. Her heraldic shield is still fitted at the bow suggesting this is a pre-war photograph. She has her modified bows and raked funnel cap.

Blücher was now cut off. Her rudder was jammed to port, so that the port engine had to be stopped and the starboard run at full speed to prevent her swinging round onto the nearby shore. Only her centre shaft kept her moving forward and this too had to be shut down shortly afterwards and her anchor dropped to keep her from drifting.

Her midships section was well ablaze, munitions and equipment belonging to her passengers from the infantry having caught fire. Below decks, chaos reigned: the area was filled with smoke, power circuits failed, the lighting gave out, gyro compasses and communications equipment was out of action. All gun crews were now mustered to fight fires but the sheer intensity of the blaze and danger from exploding ammunition, grenades and other ordnance made fire-fighting doubly hazardous. Her list of about 18 degrees was not at first too threatening but one of her 10.5cm flak ammunition magazines suddenly exploded, the blast rupturing the bulkheads between her boiler rooms and tearing open her fuel bunkers. The fuel ignited and her list gradually increased. It rapidly became clear that *Blücher* could not be saved, and the order was given to abandon ship. Some of the crew managed to reach the nearby shore through the freezing, oil-covered water, but many were lost when, at 0730hrs, she rolled over and capsized.

SCHWERE KREUZER PRINZ EUGEN

The name

The third vessel in the *Hipper* class was named for Prince Eugene of Savoy (1663–1736), a French-born statesman who departed France at the age of 20 and transferred his loyalty to Austria. Displaying considerable skills as a soldier in the Austrian army, by the age of just 30 years he had reached the rank of Feldmarschall and three years later became commander in chief of the army. In the early part of the 18th century, he secured a number of significant victories over the French armies during the War of the Spanish Succession, and ten years later provided the House of Hapsburg with a major victory over the Turks at Peterwardein before conquering Belgrade in 1717.

Without doubt the greatest of Austria's soldier-statesmen, he provided inspiration for some of the great historical figures that would follow, including Hitler's favourite historical personality, Frederick the Great.

Armorial crest

The emblem of the *Prinz Eugen* was the original crest of Prince Eugene of Savoy. This extremely complex design consisted of a traditional quartered shield. The top left was quartered once again and showed at top left a white field bearing a green cross. In each of the white quarters created by this green cross was a further smaller green cross. At top right was a red lion rampant on a blue/white-striped field; at bottom right was a further red lion rampant, crowned, on a white field and facing left. At bottom left was yet another red crowned lion rampant, this time facing right, on a yellow field. The bottom left quarter was divided vertically, with a white field with black pattern on the left and a plain black field on the right. On the white field, facing left, was a crowned black lion rampant. On the black field was a white crowned lion rampant, also facing left. The bottom right quarter was also divided vertically with, at left, a blue and yellow diced field and, at right, a white field with a red horizontal bar at the top. The top right quarter shows a white field with red pattern and, to the left, a curved draped portion in red with a white horse rampant and at right a curved draped portion with black/yellow horizontal stripes over which ran a series of green fleur-de-lis motifs. Superimposed in the centre of the crest was a smaller shield, divided vertically with a red field bearing a white cross on the left and a blue field edged in red on the right. In the top portion of the blue field were two small white fleur-de-lis. In the bottom of this field was a larger single white fleur-de-lis. The two areas were separated by a slanted red bar. *Prinz Eugen*'s crest was certainly one of the most complex armorial designs carried by a German warship.

PRINZ EUGEN SPECIFICATIONS

Length	207.7m
Beam	21.9m
Draught	7.95m
Maximum displacement	19,042 tons
Main armament	8 x 20.3cm guns in four twin turrets
Secondary armament	12 x 10.5cm guns in six twin turrets
Flak armament	12 x 3.7cm guns in six twin turrets
	8 x 2cm guns on single mounts
Torpedoes	12 x 53.3cm torpedo tubes in four triple mounts
Aircraft	3 x Arado 196 floatplanes
Complement	50 officers and 1,500 men

Ship's commanders

Kapitän zur See Helmuth Brinkmann August 1940–August 1942
Korvettenkapitän Wilhelm Beck August 1942–October 1942
Kapitän zur See Hans-Erich Voss October 1942–February 1943
Kapitän zur See Werner Ehrhardt March 1943–January 1944
Kapitän zur See Hansjürgen Reinicke January 1944–May 1945

General construction data

Prinz Eugen was protected by a partially armoured main deck, ranging from 12mm to 25mm in thickness. The armoured deck, one deck below, was some 30mm thick. The main belt of the hull, referred to as the 'citadel', had side armour 80mm thick, reducing to 40mm towards the bow and 70mm towards the stern. The turrets for the main armament had 70mm thick walls, with frontal armour 160mm thick, and a rear wall 90mm thick on turrets 'Anton' and 'Dora' and 60mm thick on 'Bruno' and 'Caesar'. The only major difference between *Prinz Eugen* and her sisters was in the form and shape of her keel and anti-torpedo bulge.

Modifications

As launched, *Prinz Eugen* featured a straight stem, and had her bow anchors set two to port and one to starboard, emerging from hawse pipes in the hullside. She also lacked any form of funnel cap. Before being accepted into the Kriegs-marine, she had her straight stem replaced by a clipper bow and a raked funnel cap fitted. Her anchor arrangement was

Decked with bunting and the national war flag, *Prinz Eugen* slides down the slipway during her launch ceremony. Note the temporary wooden walkways erected around the superstructure, and the screening over the open barbette for turret 'Anton'.

also altered to bring her into line with her sisters, with just one bow anchor to port and one to starboard, sitting at an anchor cluse each side of the bow. *Prinz Eugen* also had a prominent degaussing coil running along the hull just below the lower row of portholes.

Although when launched she featured her crests on shields either side of the bow, as opposed to a single shield on the straight stem as with *Admiral Hipper*, both shields were removed after commissioning but before she saw active service, as was the large metal eagle on her transom.

The sleek form of *Prinz Eugen* lies alongside the jetty at Gotenhafen. Interestingly, the shield-shaped mounts for the heraldic crests can still be seen at the bows, although the crests themselves have long since been removed. The radar array on her foretop rangefinder can also be seen here.

Powerplant

Prinz Eugen was driven by three Germaniawerft steam turbine engines, one mounted on the ship's centre line and one each to port and starboard. The aftmost (central) engine was located in line with the aft control centre whilst the port and starboard engines were just forward of the line of the mainmast. Each of the three propeller shafts was fitted with a three-blade propeller some 4m in diameter. A single centrally-mounted rudder was fitted and was electrically steered.

A total of 12 LaMont-type boilers were installed on *Admiral Hipper*, two to port and two to starboard in each of three boiler rooms situated from a point just ahead of the engine room for the central engine, and reaching to a point in line with the rear of the forward control centre. These produced a working pressure of 85 atmospheres.

In addition, *Prinz Eugen* was provided with four 150kW diesel generators, four 460kW turbo generators and a single 230kW turbo generator to provide for her considerable demand for electrical power, a slightly smaller generating capacity than that provided for her two older sisters.

Radar

Prinz Eugen was equipped with FuMO 27 radar sets with the 2m x 4m mattress antenna, on the foretop rangefinder housing and on the rangefinder on the aft control centre. These were carried from 1940 to 1942. Some time in September 1942, after her participation in the 'Channel Dash', her foretop radar was extended to include a new radar housing atop the rangefinder for a FuMO 26 set with 2m x 4m antenna whilst below this sat a *Timor* antenna for the FuMB 4 *Samos* passive radar detector system, the latter installed in mid-1944. FuMB 4 equipment was also installed on the mainmast. FuMB 1 and FuMB 10 *Borkum* equipment was carried on the foretop rail, and FuMB 9 *Cypern* on the foretop itself. FuMB 26 *Tunis* receivers were carried on the foretop radar housing.

A stern view of *Prinz Eugen* as she departs Gotenhafen. Note the propeller boom, swung out from the hullside just above the degaussing coil line towards the stern. This prevented the ship from swinging in against the jetty wall when moored, and thus avoided potential damage to the propeller blades.

In the final part of the war *Prinz Eugen* carried a large 3m x 6m mattress antenna for the FuMO 26 set on her foretop. In addition, an antenna was fitted to the foremast for the advanced FuMO 81 Berlin 6cm wavelength reconnaissance radar and a FuMO 25 antenna mounted on a platform on her mainmast. Certainly *Prinz Eugen* was one of the best-equipped German warships as far as radar was concerned.

Colour schemes and camouflage

As completed, *Prinz Eugen* wore the standard early pale grey livery of Kriegsmarine warships. In 1941, whilst exercising in the Baltic, she received the same pattern of disruptive camouflage paintwork as all other ships operating in this area, including the *Bismarck*. This consisted of a darker grey area to the bow and stern intended to give the impression of a shorter length, as a false bow wave was painted at the juncture of the dark forward section and the main pale grey hull. Large, wide black and white splinter stripes were also painted on the hull side and superstructure. This scheme was painted out before she set off on Operation Rheinübung with the *Bismarck*, the ship reverting to a basic pale grey finish.

From mid-1941 to mid-1942, *Prinz Eugen* featured a disruptive splinter pattern in dark grey over her base pale grey livery, but from 1943 to the end of the war reverted to overall pale grey once again. From 1941 onwards, her turret roofs were painted red. On the forecastle was painted a large red band with white disc and black swastika, simulating the Nazi flag, as a form of aerial recognition.

Pre-war service

The *Prinz Eugen* was laid down at the Krupp-Germania yard in Kiel on 23 April 1936, just six months after the contract for her manufacture was placed. Construction of the basic hull and superstructure took 28 months, the ship finally being launched on 22 August 1938. Shortly before completion, *Prinz Eugen* was hit during an RAF bombing raid on Kiel, though the damage was not too serious. On 1 August 1940, almost exactly two years after her launch, she was finally commissioned into the Kriegsmarine.

The remaining months of 1940 were spent on trials in the Baltic. Gunnery training took up the first few weeks of 1941 before the cruiser went back into dry dock for last-minute modifications and improvements. In April, *Prinz Eugen* returned to the Baltic, this time to carry out training manoeuvres along with the battleship *Bismarck*. The cruiser had been selected to accompany *Bismarck* on a commerce raid into the Atlantic. Luck was against the heavy cruiser once again, however, when on 23 April she was being escorted into the Kielerförde. British aircraft had laid mines in the waters, one of which detonated just a few metres off her starboard bow as she passed. Considerable damage was caused, most significantly a rupture to one of her fuel tanks, damage to delicate electrical equipment and to one of the cruiser's propeller shaft couplings. The proposed sortie with the *Bismarck* was postponed whilst essential repairs were made to *Prinz Eugen*. On 11 May, *Prinz Eugen* was finally ready for sea once again and moved to Gotenhafen where she would make final preparations for her fateful mission.

Wartime service

Prinz Eugen sailed on 18 May, joining the *Bismarck* at Cap Arcona, and the two made their way westward, escorted by destroyers and with strong air cover. Unfortunately for the Germans, the hope that they would pass undetected was in vain. On 20 May, the German force was spotted by a neutral Swedish warship, whose report of the sighting was intercepted by British radio monitors. Thereafter the British expended considerable effort in keeping track of the German group and they were spotted by British aircraft in Kalvenes Bay on 21 May.

On the following day, the escorting destroyers were released and the two heavy units continued on alone, shielded to some degree by heavy mist. By the evening of the next day, the weather had closed down so much that the two ships could not keep each other in sight, even though they were only a few hundred metres apart. Rounding the northern tip of Iceland, the two turned south to run down through the Denmark Strait on 23 May. At this point they were detected on radar by two patrolling British cruisers, the *Norfolk* and *Suffolk*. A few well-placed salvos from the *Bismarck* ensured that the British cruisers kept their distance, and the two continued to track the Germans by radar. In worsening weather conditions, the British cruisers mistakenly thought that the *Bismarck* was turning back towards them and retreated. By the time they realised their mistake and turned back to follow the German force again, contact had been lost.

Meanwhile, powerful British navy forces were being marshalled to hunt down the German group, the nearest of which were the battleship *Prince of Wales*

A view down into the bridge area of *Prinz Eugen*. This is the main open bridge, not the enclosed admiral's bridge up on the tower mast. This shot is taken from the roof of the forward command centre. The long tubular object in view at the base of the photograph is the housing for the rangefinder optics.

A view from astern with *Prinz Eugen's* main armament trained out to starboard. The puffs of smoke are too small to be caused by firing of the main armament and seem to have come from the 10.5cm flak guns, the barrels of which are visible in the space between the gun barrels of turrets 'Caesar' and 'Dora'.

and battlecruiser *Hood*, at that point sailing off the south-east tip of Iceland and closing fast.

On 24 May at around 0537hrs, the German ships detected the approach of enemy warships, but assumed the hydrophone contacts to be the two cruisers that had shadowed them earlier. In fact, it was the *Hood* and the *Prince of Wales* that were fast approaching.

At 0553hrs, *Hood* opened fire with her 15-inch main armament, but made the fatal mistake of aiming her shots at the lead German ship, *Prinz Eugen*, mistaking her for the *Bismarck*. The German cruiser answered with a full broadside from her 20.3cm armament, first straddling the British warship and, by the third salvo, scoring direct hits. *Prinz Eugen* then turned her guns on the *Prince of Wales* as the *Bismarck* started to shoot at the *Hood*. Almost immediately, a direct hit was scored on the *Hood* just forward of her aft main armament. A few seconds later, at 0601hrs, just eight minutes after the action began, *Hood* was torn apart by a massive internal explosion. Her magazines having detonated and her back broken, she sank immediately taking 1,416 crewmen to the bottom with her. Both German ships now turned their armament on the *Prince of Wales*, which suffered several hits before turning away. Firing ceased at 0609hrs. In just 16 minutes of furious action, the pride of the Royal Navy had been sunk and one of its newest battleships severely damaged.

Bismarck, though she had suffered no fatal injury, had been damaged enough to reduce her effectiveness, a hit near the bows causing serious flooding, which resulted in a bows-down attitude and reduced speed. This also rendered part of her fuel supply inaccessible, and resulted in a fuel leak at the bows, which would make tracking her so much easier for the enemy.

The group commander, Admiral Lütjens, decided to end the sortie in view of the damage to the flagship, and to make for a friendly port in occupied France. *Prinz Eugen*, totally unscathed, was to be released to carry on alone. On 26 May, she rendezvoused with an oil tanker and took on fuel to top up her nearly empty bunkers. The cruiser, however, was suffering from problems caused by contaminated fuel and engine room machinery faults, steam leaks, damaged propeller blades and turbine bearing problems, all of which led to the decision to abandon the remainder of the mission and make for port.

On 31 May, having been met by an escort force of destroyers, *Prinz Eugen* put into Brest where she remained bottled up for the next eight months undergoing repairs. Here she was in constant danger from Allied air attack and indeed, on 2 July, was damaged by British bombers. Over 100 crewmembers were killed or injured in the raid.

Brest became home to three Kriegsmarine heavy units, with *Scharnhorst* and *Gneisenau* bottled up in the port with *Prinz Eugen*.

Constant Allied air raids were becoming ever more problematic. Eventually, Grossadmiral Raeder's hopes of using the squadron on a raiding sortie into the Atlantic were squashed when Hitler ordered the ships home to Germany. Raeder was horrified to learn that not only were the ships being ordered home, but that Hitler had specified that they proceed by way of the English Channel, right under the noses of the Royal Navy, depending for safety on the element of surprise. Protests were met with the Führer's insistence that the ships either return home via the Channel as ordered, or that he would have them paid off and remove their weapons for use on land.

Under cover of darkness on 11 February 1942, the German warships, with a substantial escort of destroyers and torpedo boats, put to sea. The ships made good progress, unnoticed by British submarine patrols and undetected by British radar. Heavy air cover arrived at dawn and it was not until the force was off Le Touquet that they were spotted by British reconnaissance aircraft, and even then were misidentified as a merchant convoy. Once the ships were properly identified, and the British realised they had been caught on the hop, a number of hastily organised sorties were organised in an attempt to stop the Germans. *Prinz Eugen* came under fire from the British shore batteries near Dover, though all of the shots fell short and the cruiser remained undamaged. Shortly thereafter, a number of motor torpedo boats appeared on the scene but were driven off by the *Prinz Eugen*'s destroyer escorts. No sooner had they departed than a number of Swordfish torpedo-carrying aircraft appeared on the scene. Fortunately for the Germans, no hits were scored. Four of the aircraft were shot down and the remainder driven off. This was to be the first of several air attacks, none of which was to cause any damage to the cruiser. Just before 1645hrs, British destroyers were spotted and *Prinz Eugen* opened fire with her main armament. A number of hits were scored on the enemy but the heavy cruiser was forced to manoeuvre violently to avoid a spread of torpedoes. Although numerous further air attacks were mounted against the German force, *Prinz Eugen* reached Brunsbüttel safely on the morning of 13 February.

One week later, accompanied by the *Admiral Scheer*, the *Prinz Eugen* sailed for Norway, stopping briefly at Grimstadtfjord before continuing the journey onwards to Trondheim. On the morning of 23 February, *Prinz Eugen* was spotted by the British submarine HMS *Trident*. A torpedo fired by the submarine hit *Prinz Eugen*'s stern, killing and injuring several of the crew, causing severe damage and blowing off her rudder. The heavy cruiser was rendered unmanoeuvrable. *Prinz Eugen* was taken into Lofjord where emergency repairs were effected. These consisted of removing her entire stern, plating over the gaping hole and installing a large manually operated capstan on the quarterdeck to allow her to be steered. Despite Allied air attacks on her during her return voyage to Germany, *Prinz Eugen* reached Kiel on 18 May without receiving further damage.

View over *Prinz Eugen*'s bow area, taken during the 'Channel Dash'. Note the quadruple-barrelled *Flakvierling* mounted on the forecastle and on the roof of turret 'Bruno'.

The ship was out of service for six months, finally returning to sea on 27 October. She spent the next two months undergoing trials in the Baltic and, having proven herself fully fit for service, was ordered to return to Norwegian waters in early January 1943 in the company of battleship *Scharnhorst*. In the event, the German ships were spotted by British aircraft, and with the element of surprise lost it was decided that it would be too dangerous to continue. Both ships returned to port. A second attempt on 25 January was also abandoned.

Thereafter, *Prinz Eugen* was allocated to the Fleet Training Squadron and for the next nine months was used on cadet training exercises in the Baltic.

On 1 October, she was re-assigned to active service duties, the intent being to use her for shore support duties as the situation on the Eastern Front worsened. In June 1944, *Prinz Eugen* was sent to the Gulf of Finland to help cover the German withdrawal. In August, she was dispatched to the Gulf of Riga where she was used for bombardment of Soviet positions near Tukkum supported by four destroyers, with even the ship's Arado floatplanes being committed to action. In early September, after this successful action, *Prinz Eugen* returned to the Gulf of Finland to support an attempt, ultimately unsuccessful, to seize the Finnish fortress island of Hogland. By mid-month she was in Gotenhafen once again, having taken no part in the action. In late September, however, she made a more meaningful contribution to the war effort by escorting a convoy of German ships that were evacuating German troops from the base at Kemi in Finland to safety in Danzig.

On 11 October, *Prinz Eugen* was once again in action, giving fire support to beleaguered German troops in Memel, where she fired off well over 600 rounds from her main armament. Two days later she returned, having replenished her ammunition supplies, and fired off another 370 rounds. On completion of this operation, *Prinz Eugen* was steaming at full speed along the approaches to the port of Gotenhafen when she rammed the light cruiser *Leipzig* almost exactly amidships, nearly cutting her in half. *Prinz Eugen* was wedged fast into *Leipzig*'s hull and remained there until the next day when the two were separated. The damaged heavy cruiser was taken into Gotenhafen for repairs, which were rapidly effected, and the ship was once again seaworthy in just one month.

Almost as soon as she was ready for action, *Prinz Eugen* was again assigned to shore support work, attacking Soviet positions on Sworbe in the Gulf of Riga, firing over 500 rounds of 20.3cm ammunition. Her ammunition exhausted, she returned to Gotenhafen where she went into dock for refitting whilst her worn-out main armament barrels were re-bored.

Prinz Eugen was declared ready for action again in mid-January 1945, by which time the situation on the Eastern Front was desperate. At the end of that month, she was once again tasked with shore

View forward from the roof of the rangefinder housing atop the forward command centre. Ahead of *Prinz Eugen*, travelling in line astern, are the battleships *Scharnhorst* and *Gneisenau*.

bombardment work, this time against Soviet troops on German soil. Over 870 rounds of 20.3cm ammunition were fired at enemy forces around Cranz, near Königsberg, though by now the Soviet advance was unstoppable and the massive firepower of the *Prinz Eugen* could offer only temporary relief to the German defenders. Critical shortages of ammunition meant that *Prinz Eugen* could not go into action again until March when she bombarded Soviet forces around Gotenhafen, Zoppot, Danzig and Hela.

On 10 April, the situation having deteriorated to the extent that *Prinz Eugen* could no longer have any appreciable effect, she departed the Baltic and made her way westwards, reaching Copenhagen on 20 April. She was officially decommissioned on 7 May and handed over to the Royal Navy on 8 May.

Prinz Eugen's career was not quite over, however. In December 1945 she was handed over to the Americans and was actually commissioned into the US Navy and sailed to the USA by her original crew. Once the US Navy had learned all they needed to learn from examination of the ship and had no further need for her, she was towed to Bikini Atoll in the Marshall Islands and anchored alongside a number of obsolete and unneeded American warships. Here, on 1 July, an atomic bomb was exploded during the US test programme. *Prinz Eugen* survived this test and a subsequent one on 25 July but was so heavily contaminated by radiation that she could not be considered for any further use. She was towed to Wajalein Atoll where, on 22 December 1946, she capsized and sank.

Also taken during the 'Channel Dash', this view from the bow shows *Prinz Eugen* rolling in heavy seas. The Flakvierling on the forecastle and its crew can be clearly seen.

SCHWERE KREUZER SEYDLITZ

The fourth heavy cruiser in the *Hipper* class was named after Friedrich Wilhelm von Seydlitz (1721–73), a highly successful Prussian general who came to the fore as a colonel in command of a squadron of cavalry during the Seven Years War, winning several inspiring victories against superior enemy forces and without infantry support. He was eventually appointed inspector general of cavalry and to the rank of General der Kavallerie in 1767.

The *Seydlitz* was laid down at the Deschimag Yard in Bremen on 29 December 1936, five months after the contract for her manufacture was placed. Construction of the basic hull and superstructure took just over two years, the ship finally being launched on 19 January 1939. She was never commissioned into the Kriegsmarine, a decision being made in June 1942 to convert the partially completed hull into an aircraft carrier. Turrets 'Bruno' and 'Caesar' had already been installed and were subsequently removed. The hull was transferred to Königsberg for completion as a carrier and work continued at a slow pace until January 1943 when it was finally halted. Never completed, *Seydlitz* was scuttled in January 1945 as the Red Army approached Königsberg.

SCHWERE KREUZER LÜTZOW

The final ship in the *Hipper* class to be laid down was named for Adolf, Freiherr von Lützow (1782–1843). Lützow entered military service as a mere 13-year-old boy, and by 1806 at the battle of Auerstedt was a commissioned Leutnant. He was a major figure in the opposition to Napoleon and in 1813 was tasked with raising a volunteer force to oppose the French. He achieved this with considerable success, ultimately fielding some 3,500 mixed infantry, mounted personnel and artillery. His force suffered heavy casualties in its guerrilla actions against the French, however, and was ultimately disbanded. Lützow was given command of a cavalry regiment with the rank of Oberstleutnant, and by 1822 had reached the rank of Generalmajor. He retired from military service in 1830.

Prinz Eugen's bow plunges into the waves. Most of the German heavy units were known as 'wet' ships, despite the clipper bow modifications.

The *Lützow* was laid down at the Deschimag Yard in Bremen on 2 August 1937, the contract for her construction having been issued at the same time as that for *Seydlitz*. Construction of the basic hull and superstructure took just under two years, the ship finally being launched on 1 July 1939. Like *Seydlitz*, she was never completed, her partially finished hull being sold to the Soviet Union in April 1940. The only armament installed was turret 'Anton' and the superstructure itself still lacked a funnel and other major components. The Soviets towed the ship to Leningrad where it was taken into the Red Navy and renamed as *Petropavlovsk*. The name Lützow was subsequently allocated to the pocket battleship *Deutschland* when it was considered necessary to re-name her.

By the commencement of Operation Barbarossa in July 1941, the ship had still not been completed, now sporting only one further forward main turret. She was damaged by German artillery fire in September 1941, and then in April 1942 Luftwaffe bombing raids damaged her so severely that she sank, grounding in shallow waters. Raised in September of that year, she was used as a floating gun battery giving much-needed artillery support to Soviet forces on the Leningrad Front. Later renamed the *Tallin*, she survived the war and was finally scrapped in 1960 after spending some time as an accommodation hulk.

BIBLIOGRAPHY

Breyer, Siegfried, and Koop, Gerhard, *The German Navy at War, Vol 1*, Schiffer Publishing, West Chester, 1989

Gröner, Erich, *Die deutschen Kriegsschiffe 1815–1945*, Bernard & Graefe Munich, 1982

Koop, Gerhard, and Schmolke, Klaus-Peter, *Heavy Cruisers of the Admiral Hipper Class*, Greenhill Books, London, 2001

Whitley, Michael, *German Cruisers of World War 2*, London, 1985

COLOUR PLATE COMMENTARY

A: *ADMIRAL HIPPER*

1 *Admiral Hipper* as first completed. She has the early straight stem, with her heraldic crest mounted on the stem itself, though this was later moved to the side of the bows. She also still features the large cast bronze eagle emblem on her stern. The later, very distinctive, raked funnel cap has not yet been fitted and her anchor is still in the hullside anchor hawse. Overall colour scheme is pale grey, and as would be expected in peacetime, she is in pristine condition.

  2 Bow view showing the ship's crest as it was originally completed, mounted on the straight stem.

  3 Revised 'clipper' bow with distinct rake. Note also the swastika flag painted on the foredeck for aerial recognition purposes.

  4 The revised tower structure showing the enclosed glazed bridge area and FuMo radar mounted on the foretop fire control housing.

  5 The original tower structure with open-topped bridge and searchlight platform, the searchlight being replaced later by an additional flak gun position.

  6 Midships view showing the funnel as originally completed before the distinctive raked cap was fitted.

B: *ADMIRAL HIPPER* IN ACTION

View from astern of *Admiral Hipper* in action during the final part of the war. This angle gives a good view of her rear superstructure, showing the fire control director and the two flak fire control towers with their distinctive spherical domed tops. Note also the additional 3.7cm flak mounting on the roof of turret 'Caesar'.

  Also seen here are the searchlights mounted at the base of the mainmast and the mainmast radar antenna.

  Admiral Hipper was one of the more successful heavy units. During her war cruise of April 1941, she sank between seven and 14 enemy ships (the exact number differing depending on the source consulted) making her by far the most successful vessel of her class.

Prinz Eugen pictured in the Baltic port of Gotenhafen later in the war. She is sporting a much darker shade of grey than that usually featured earlier in the war.

C: *BLÜCHER*

1 Here we see *Blücher* as first commissioned into the Kriegsmarine. She still has the straight stem, but already had the anchors moved from the hullside hawse apertures into a cluse on the side of the forecastle. One anchor is carried to each side with a third on the stem itself. She still lacks the funnel cap, which would shortly be fitted, and has only basic rangefinder equipment, no radar having been installed at this point. The colour scheme is overall pale grey and her heraldic crests have already been moved to the side of the bow.

  2 Blücher in her early days had her anchor set into hawse holes on the hull side, with two anchors to port and one to standard. Her heraldic shield was mounted on the stem.

  3 The original stem was later refitted to give the cruiser a steeply raked 'clipper' bow. At this time her anchor's arrangement was altered to just one anchor each side, set into a cluse on the forecastle.

  4 The stern featured an anchor on the port side only, this being set into a shaped recess on the stern.

  5 This inset shows the later distinctive raked funnel cap, which was fitted to *Blücher* shortly after her completion.

D: *PRINZ EUGEN* CUTAWAY

The basic design layout of the *Admiral Hipper*-class heavy cruisers was fairly conventional, with its eight-gun main armament laid out in four twin turrets, two facing forward and two aft. Unlike the situation on battleships and pocket battleships, there was no smaller calibre secondary armament, but this was a fairly conventional arrangement. Instead, the 10.5cm heavy flak guns were capable of being used against surface as well as aerial targets.

Their journey over, the army's mountain troops look back towards *Admiral Hipper* as they are ferried to the shore.

The 212.5-metre-long hull (205.9m for *Prinz Eugen* shown here) was divided into 14 compartments. The hull was double bottomed and of welded construction. For the main part of the ship, below the main deck were two further deck levels, the so-called battery deck and the armoured deck. Below this were the turbine and boiler rooms.

A single funnel was provided, located amidships and directly above the boiler rooms, of which in *Prinz Eugen* there were six, each with four boilers, and from which led massive gas trunking pipes up into the funnel. Forward of the boiler room area was the forward electrical power plant containing diesel-electric and turbo generators. Immediately astern of the boiler rooms lay the turbine room containing the two Germaniawerft turbines that drove the outboard propeller shafts. Astern of this large compartment was a further electricity generating room containing further diesel-electric and turbo generators. Moving further astern

was the turbine room containing the Germaniawerft turbine that drove the centrally mounted propeller shaft, and finally a third electrical power generating room with both diesel-electric and turbo generators.

The lower levels of the hull forward and aft of the main superstructure and adjacent to the turret shafts held the ammunition magazines for the 20.3cm shells.

As can be imagined with a crew of between 1,400 and 1,600 men at any one time, a good proportion of the ship was given over to crew accommodation, the crew being divided into ten divisions. Divisions 1 to 4 were seamen, 5 to 7 were engine-room personnel, 8 was gunners, 9 was signal and communications personnel and 10 was general administrative personnel.

In common with the design of several other classes of heavy ships, the *Hipper* class had their forward command centre with a distinctive 'tower' mast (*Turmmast*) comprising the forward superstructure. In this they were similar to the *Scharnhorst* class and especially to the *Bismarck* class which the cruisers very closely resembled visually – and indeed they were on occasion erroneously identified as their bigger cousins by Allied reconnaissance aircraft. Again, a common feature was the location of rangefinder equipment on the foretop and on the roof of the forward command centre. Aft of the funnel was the aircraft hangar, and beyond that the aft control centre, also with its rangefinder equipment. All of these features were common to the battleships as well as heavy cruisers. In many ways the *Hipper*-class cruisers were almost like smaller versions of the *Bismarck*-class battleships. Few other navies possessed warships where two distinctly different classes resembled each other quite so closely.

Another common design feature was the positioning of the flak fire control equipment, in spherical housings, one to each side of the main tower mast complex and one either side of the mainmast. These fed data down to command

A beautiful shot of *Admiral Hipper,* as completed. Amongst points to note are the straight stem, with its heraldic crest, the lack of funnel cap, the open bridge (later enclosed), and the lack of radar equipment on the foretop rangefinder housing. Note, however, that the anchor configuration is of the later type, with the anchors sitting in a cluse on the edge of the forecastle, rather than emerging from an aperture on the hullside.

Blücher **slides down the slipway on the day of her launch. Note the straight stem and the original anchor configuration.**

posts below decks, which interpreted the data and relayed firing orders back up to the gun positions.

Hipper-class cruisers were also provided with underwater sound detection equipment (*Unterwasser-Horchgeräte*) of very high standard. It was in fact the *Prinz Eugen* equipment that first detected the approach of the *Hood* and the *Prince of Wales* during her encounter with the *Bismarck*. This equipment was built into a small bulge at the base of the stem.

The radar installation shown here reflects *Prinz Eugen's* most advanced progression in this respect, being given far more extensive radar equipment than any of her sisters, or indeed most other significant German warships of any kind.

E: *PRINZ EUGEN*

1 Prinz Eugen in profile view. The clipper bow and raked funnel cap are particularly distinctive. Note also the considerable additional flak armament, on the roof of turrets 'Bruno' and 'Caesar' as well as on the foredeck and quarterdeck.

2 *Prinz Eugen* in plan view. The basic layout remains the same as for *Admiral Hipper* and *Blücher* but, as this plan view clearly shows, her decks are liberally peppered with light flak gun positions. The large swastika emblems painted on her foredeck as aerial recognition symbols were later painted out. The Luftwaffe no longer had control of the

skies and the Kriegsmarine had no wish to advertise its identity to enemy aircraft.

3 *Prinz Eugen's* foretop. Note the extensive FuMo radar array she carried in the late stages of the war. The searchlight mounted on the platform just below the foretop has been removed and replaced by an anti-aircraft gun. Note also the steeply-raked funnel cap.

4 Turret 'Bruno' on the *Prinz Eugen*. Note the additional flak armament mounted on the turret roof and on the main deck between turrets 'Anton' and 'Bruno'.

F: *PRINZ EUGEN* IN ACTION

Prinz Eugen on shore bombardment duty in the Baltic, 1945. This bow view gives a good impression of the massive bulk of this class of heavy cruiser. *Prinz Eugen* was forced into use in shore support in a vain attempt to hold back Soviet land forces in coastal regions. The effect of shore bombardment from heavy ship's artillery should not be underestimated. The Germans themselves had suffered terribly from this during the Allied landings in Normandy and were well aware of the physical and psychological effects such bombardments could have. During operations off Königsberg in January 1945, in the course of three days, *Prinz Eugen* fired over 870 rounds of 20.3cm ammunition against Soviet held positions. Despite the weight of this and similar bombardments by other German heavy units, including *Prinz Eugen's* sister, *Admiral Hipper*, such operations could at best offer only temporary relief for the beleaguered German forces on land.

G: LATE-WAR CAMOUFLAGE SCHEMES

1 Here we see *Admiral Hipper* in a colour scheme dating from around the middle of 1944. Her pale grey base livery has a distinctive dark grey disruptive camouflage scheme painted over it. She also has more extensive FuMO radar equipment fitted and, like *Prinz Eugen* during the same period, has had her flak armament beefed up.

2 USS *Prinz Eugen* is shown here in her final appearance just before being used in the US atomic bomb test programme at Bikini Atoll in July 1946, having been sailed over to the USA by her original crew and commissioned into the US Navy under her original name. She has returned to her original pale grey overall livery and is in relatively good condition after years of heavy use. Prior to the bomb test, the guns from turret 'Anton' were removed as seen here, as was the forward starboard flak rangefinder housing, though most of her other fittings were left intact. *Prinz Eugen* survived the bomb blast but was so heavily irradiated that any plans for further use had to be abandoned.

3 This rather interesting view shows *Prinz Eugen* in the aftermath of her being torpedoed by the British submarine *Trident* in 1942. Her ruined stern and rudder has been neatly cut away and the resultant gap plated over, thus shortening her length significantly and giving her a squared-off stern. She then had to be steered manually, using a capstan set up on her quarterdeck. A very basic camouflage scheme is featured with the large part of her hull painted dark grey.

Prinz Eugen in her 'Baltic' camouflage, sported until departing from Norway on her fateful voyage with the *Bismarck.* Note the darker paint on the bow section, the white false bow wave and the black/white angular disruptive stripes further back along the hull. A disruptive scheme has also been painted on her forward turrets.

A shot of the galley on *Prinz Eugen* as one of the cooks prepares a soup or stew.

INDEX

Achates, HMS 18
Admiral Hipper 9–21, 44, **45**, **A**
  in action **4**, 12–21, **12**, **19**, 44, **45**, **B**
  bow view **10**
  bridge to stern **8**
  colours and camouflage 12, **16**, **19**, 44, 47, **A**, **F**
  commanders 10
  crest 9, 11, 44, **45**, **A**
  description and equipment 10–12
  fitting out **13**
  forward superstructure **14**
  guns and gunners **4**, **5**, **6**, 11
  midships **15**
  modified **11**
  quarterdeck **17**
  specifications 10
  stern **18**
Admiral Scheer 17, 40
aerial recognition symbols **33**, 46, **E**
aircraft catapults **8**
anchors and capstans
  Admiral Hipper **18**, 22, **45**
  Blücher 23, **23**, **33**, 44, **46**, **C**
  Prinz Eugen 35–6
Anglo-German Naval Treaty (1935) 5
armour 10, 35
Atlantic operations 15–16, 38–9
atomic bomb tests 42, 47

Baltic operations 41–2, 46, **F**
Bismarck 38–9
Blücher 21–34, **21**, 44, **C**
  in action 23–34, **34**
  bow configuration **23**
  colours and camouflage 23, 44, **C**
  commanders 22
  crest 22, **22**, **33**, 44, **C**
  description and equipment 23
  fitting out **20**
  launch 22, **46**
  specifications 22
  during trials **19**, **22**, **24**
  turret to bow **33**
Blücher, Generalfeldmarschall Gebhard Leberecht Fürst von Wahlstatt **3**, 21
boilers and boiler rooms 11, 23, 36, 45, **D**
bows, clipper **20**, **22**, **33**, 44, 46, **A**, **C**, **E**
Bramble, HMS 18
Bremse 7
bridges 38, 44, **45**, **A**
British convoys
  JW 51B 17–20
  PQ17 17

camouflage *see* colour schemes and camouflage
cap ribbons **3**
'Channel Dash' **40**, **40**, 42
colour schemes and camouflage
  Admiral Hipper 12, **16**, **19**, 44, 47, **A**, **F**
  Blücher 23, 44, **C**

Prinz Eugen 37, **44**, 47, **47**, **F**
construction and fitting out
  Admiral Hipper 12, **13**
  Blücher **20**, 22
  Prinz Eugen 37
crests and shields, heraldic
  Admiral Hipper 9, 11, 44, **45**, **A**
  Blücher 22, **22**, **33**, 44, **C**
  Prinz Eugen 34–5, 36, **36**
crew **6**, **10**, **21**, 45

decks 10, 35, 45, **D**
degaussing coils 36, **37**
design layout 44–6, **D**

emblems, eagle 18, 36, 44, **A**
engines 11, 23, 36, 45, **D**
Ester Thorden 15
Eugene of Savoy, Prince **3**, 34

floatplanes **7**, **9**, 41
Friedrich Eckoldt 14, 17–18, 19
funnels and funnel caps 45, **D**
  Admiral Hipper **8**, 11, **11**, 44, **45**, **A**
  Blücher **19**, **21**, **22**, 23, **24**, **33**, 44, **C**
  Prinz Eugen 35, 46, **E**

galleys 47
Gebirgsjäger **4**, **12**, 45
German navy, treaties limiting 3–5
Gesellschaft für Elektroakustische und Mechanische Apparate (GEMA) 7–8
Glowworm, HMS 13
Gneisenau 13, 14, 16, 39, **41**
guns 5–7
  2cm flak **6**, **40**, **42**
  3.7cm flak **6**, 44, **B**
  4cm Bofors flak 6–7
  10.5cm flak **5**, **6**, **8**, **39**, 44, **D**<
  20.3cm **4**, 5–6
  anti-aircraft 46, **E**
  fire control and rangefinders 8–9, **8**, **11**, **14**, **15**, **38**, 44, 45–6, **B**–**D**
  flak **12**, **14**, 46, **E**
  flak platforms **15**
  layout 44, **D**

Hipper, Adm. Franz Ritter von **3**, 9
Hitler, Adolf 20, 40
Hood, HMS 38–9
hulls 10, 35, 45, **D**

Jamaica, HMS 18

Köln 17, 20
Kummetz, Adm. 17, 18, 24

life vests **6**
London Naval Agreement (1930) 5
Lützow (heavy cruiser) 43
Lützow (pocket battleship) 17, 19, 24, 33
Lützow, Adolf, Freiherr von 43

Norway operations **4**, **12**, 13–14, **19**, 24–34, 40–1, **45**

Obdurate, HMS 18
Obedient, HMS 18
Onslow, HMS 18
Operation Rösselsprung 17
Orwell, HMS 18

Prince of Wales, HMS 38–9
Prinz Eugen 34–42, **36**, **44**, 46, **E**
  in action 17, 37–42, **40**–**2**, 46, **F**
  armament **7**, **7**, **39**
  bow **40**, **43**
  from bow **42**
  bridge **38**
  colours and camouflage 37, **44**, 47, **47**, **F**
  commanders 35
  crest 34–5, 36, **36**
  cutaway 44–6, **D**
  description and equipment 35–7
  floatplanes **9**
  galley 47
  launch 35, 37
  specifications 35
  stern 37
  view forward **41**
propeller booms 37

radar 7–8
  Admiral Hipper 11–12, **11**, **16**, 44, **A**, **B**
  Blücher 23
  Prinz Eugen 36–7, **36**, 46, **D**, **E**
Raeder, Adm. 7, 12, 20, 40
Richard Beitzen 17–18, 19

Scapa Flow 3
Scharnhorst 13, 14, ●●, 39, 41, **41**
searchlights and platforms **14**, 44, **A**, **B**
Seydlitz 42
Seydlitz, Friedrich Wilhelm von 42
Sheffield, HMS 18
sound detection equipment 46
specifications
  Admiral Hipper 10
  Blücher 22
  Prinz Eugen 35

Tirpitz 17, **19**
torpedoes and torpedo tubes **7**, **7**, **D**
tower structures 44, **A**
Trident, HMS 40
turrets 5, 10, 35
  'Anton' **8**–**9**, **D**
  'Bruno' 9, **12**, **40**, 46, **D**, **E**
  'Caesar' 9, **15**, **39**, 44, 46, **A**, **D**, **E**
  'Dora' 9, **39**, **D**

Versailles, Treaty of (1919) **4**

Washington Agreement (1922) 4–5
Welle 7